## Advanced praise for
## *What Rain Taught Us*

In *What Rain Taught Us*, Gail Ashton is at the height of her lyrical powers. But what makes this collection stand out is the marriage of experiment to musicality, and the result is an amplification of potency. This collection, brave in content and form, presents a compelling, poignant and gripping narrative of life that sizzles with truth.
    **Jane McKie**

Rain, moonlight and the words of old songs haunt these poems, with their interconnecting threads of language and unexpected twists and turns on the page. 'Think of it as a voyage', the poet tells us, and indeed by the end we have travelled a long way through the seas of the imagination.
    **Matthew Francis**

In the urgent poems of *What Rain Taught Us*, Gail Ashton tests the limits of the lines she makes, framing and reorienting the spaces around their images, examining how images fade in and out of focus, navigating her way to an understanding of the terrors the poems describe. These poems see 'the unspecified disorder of flowers', and they make us grasp, too, how 'sunlight frets/the shock of them, unfamiliar/with their dialect.'
    **John McAuliffe**

It's rare to come upon a collection of poetry that has such a gripping narrative and is simultaneously so visually audacious. At times, the text teeters across the pages, letters toppling from the ends of lines, while, at others, words form themselves into constellations, or heave and churn like waves, all the while artfully reflecting each poem's theme. Striking, often surreal, images pitter-patter through the poems, alongside sprinklings of inventive wordplay and droplets of song. *What Rain Taught Us*, teaches us that Ashton's commitment to taking risks with form, language and subject-matter has given rise to a quite extraordinary collection.
    **Susan Richardson**


An elegant, carefully ordered collection with a deep-felt narrative, although for me the story really resides in Ashton's distinctive tone, those humorous but serious conversations and intimate touches that *What Rain Taught Us* offers. Here, too, is a living and innovative conversation between poet and typographer which follows its own bold and peculiar trajectory to fly off mid-point with its text upon text, its half-hidden italics well suiting Ashton's wry tone, and, at the end, a wonderful mirror-written piece juxtaposed by an asemic pixelated background to promise very interesting follow-ups in the future.
    **Judy Kendall**

# WHAT RAIN TAUGHT US

by
Gail Ashton

L/FB 306

Published by Liquorice Fish Books, an imprint of Cinnamon Press,
Meirion House, Tanygrisiau, Blaenau Ffestiniog, Gwynedd, LL41 3SU
www.cinnamonpress.com/index.php/liquorice-fish-books/about

All rights reserved by the authors. The right of each contributor to be identified as the author of their work has been asserted by them in accordance with the Copyright, Designs and Patent Act, 1988.
Copyright © 2017 Gail Ashton.

ISBN: 978-0-9931682-8-4

British Library Cataloguing in Publication Data. A CIP record for this book can be obtained from the British Library.

All rights reserved. No part of this publication may be reproduced, stored in a retrieval system, or transmitted in any form or by any means, electronic, mechanical, photocopying, recording or otherwise without the prior written permission of the publishers. This book may not be lent, hired out, resold or otherwise disposed of by way of trade in any form of binding or cover other than that in which it is published, without the prior consent of the publishers.

Interior and exterior design and layout by Adam Craig. Front cover source image: Raindrops Water Ripples © Dave Bredson/Cameraydave | Dreamstime.com. Splash image, p. 7, from a photo by andreiapinto09 @ pixabay.com/en/water-clearn-drop-1263001, CCO Public Doman.

Printed in Poland.

Cinnamon Press is represented in the UK by Inpress Ltd www.inpressbooks.co.uk and in Wales by the Welsh Books Council www.cllc.org.uk.


**Acknowledgements**

Huge thanks to everyone who read, commented on and supported this venture: my lovely writing comrades Jenny Cooke, Frances Sackett and Sue Tyson; Judy Kendall, Jane McKie and Susan Richardson for their enthusiasm and invaluable advice; everyone at the Welsh residential especially Liz Fincham, Anne Hine, Julie Noble and Isabelle Llasera for making me laugh; my sister Nettie, Michelle and Geoff for putting up with me; and last but definitely not least Jan Fortune for her continued faith in me and the amazing 'manner of man' that is Adam Craig without whom this book would never have stepped into the light.

Some of these poems appeared in various guises in Envoi. Nothing Short (of miraculous) took third place in the Cinnamon Open Poetry Competition 2016.

'Sailing a calypso' inspired by 'Quilting for Childless Women 8. Log Cabin, Barn Raising Variation (Crib Quilt)', Gwyneth Lewis, Sparrow Tree (Bloodaxe, 2011).

'Worlds Not Solid: on how I mended my ways', takes its notions from Revelation, 2:17 and from 'What Tom Said to the Witch', Frances Spurrier, The Pilgrim's Trail (Cinnamon Press, 2014).

# CONTENTS

| | |
|---|---|
| Apparently | 11 |
| Talk of rain | 12 |
| This Tuesday's challenge: so you think you're a comedian | 14 |
| How it ends | 15 |
| What you won't tell her | 16 |
| nightingale: symptomatic | 17 |
| Are you sitting comfortably? | 18 |
| Sometimes, something, so what | 19 |
| Cataloguing catastrophe | 20 |
| being accidental (in my mother's house) | 22 |
| only nine words left | 23 |
| adventures with my house | 24 |
| No middle ground | 26 |
| the story of meeting a hero on the occasion of his 51st birthday | 27 |
| Lullaby | 28 |
| way past your bedtime | 30 |
| Think of it | 31 |
| For the journey | 32 |
| In (the) Hold | 33 |
| Stowed Away | 34 |
| Sidelined | 35 |
| Drowning | 36 |
| how | 37 |
| revelations | 38 |
| vascular | 39 |
| immortality | 40 |
| astrolabe | 41 |

| | |
|---|---|
| lamentation | 42 |
| genesis | 43 |
| bereft | 44 |
| chapters | 45 |
| reprise | 46 |
| Crossing an ocean, nightfall | 47 |
| Down | 48 |
| according to rain | 49 |
| echo location | 50 |
| Being of wonders | 51 |
| I would like to tell you that | 52 |
| Sailing a Calypso | 54 |
| A different affair altogether | 55 |
| In the lining of a pocket | 56 |
| while I was thinking on | 57 |
| Worlds Not Solid … | 58 |
| Keys | 62 |
| I saw you walking (Sky field) | 63 |
| Home | 64 |
| What rain taught us | 65 |
| singing bowl (copper, tonal) | 68 |
| in a room full of lost objects | 69 |
| a face in every upturned | 70 |
| Book of Hours | 71 |
| Nothing short (of miraculous) | 73 |
| History of the world | 74 |

*For Michelle*

# WHAT RAIN TAUGHT US

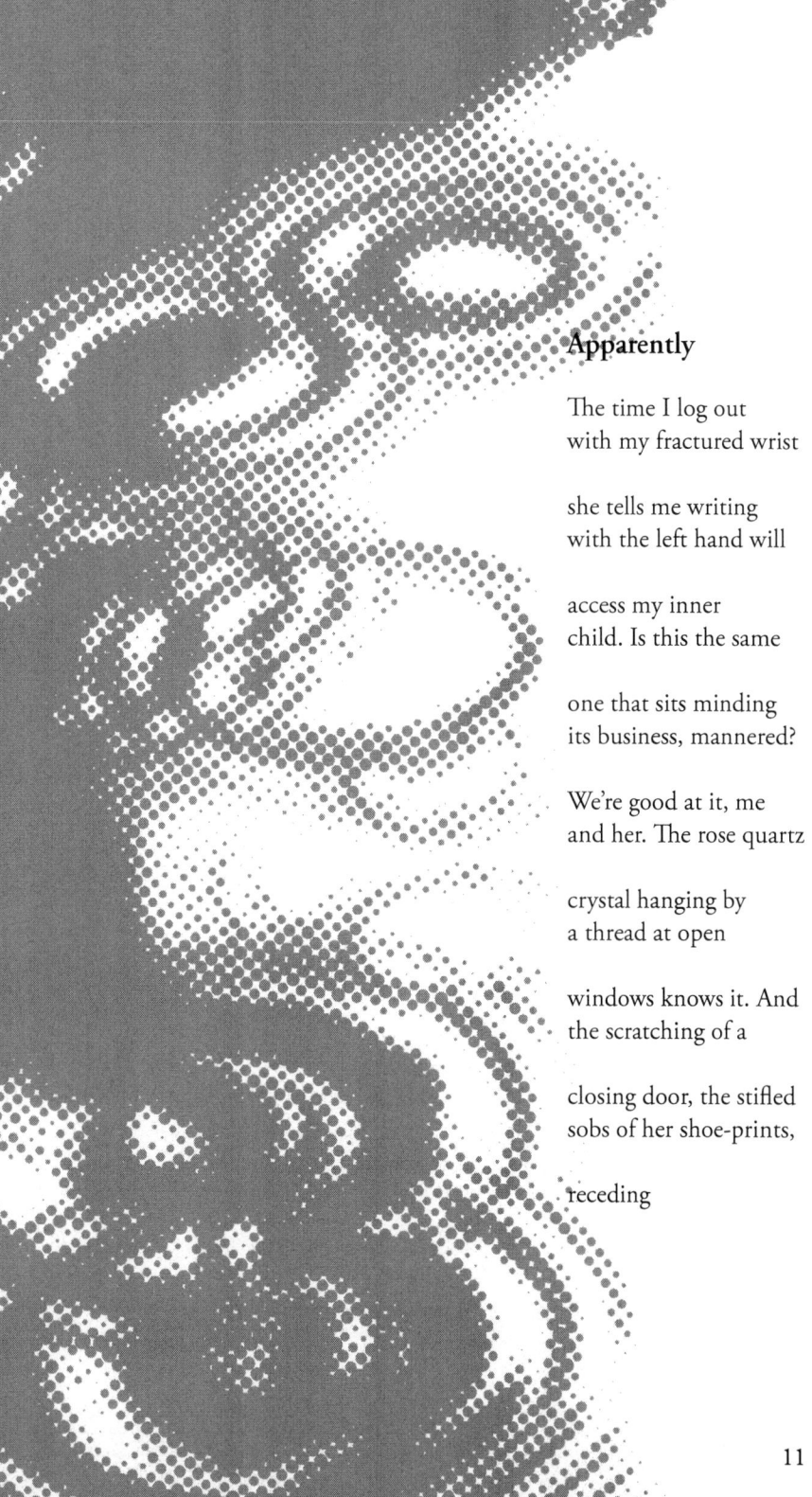

## Apparently

The time I log out
with my fractured wrist

she tells me writing
with the left hand will

access my inner
child. Is this the same

one that sits minding
its business, mannered?

We're good at it, me
and her. The rose quartz

crystal hanging by
a thread at open

windows knows it. And
the scratching of a

closing door, the stifled
sobs of her shoe-prints,

receding

# Talk of rain

I

It's how we start, a canny
ease-in on her part.

She tells me of departures
from Miami, how

in the lee of flight no-one
could catch her. I am startled

by rain in her eyes.

II

Believe in nothing
save this weather and
her bright scent, flailing.

III

My hair always wet for our appointments.

This can be cured. Not so the inside of

skin where water pearls, like ammonite.

IV

All day it swallows landmarks,
hungers at the windowpane.

I could consume her hair and
still not ignite that darkness.

This is not as lovers talk.
Just I cannot bear the flood.

V

                    Both
                our dogs
                hate rain.
           And who could
              blame them?
     I dreamed a skein of dolphins
              in our lane.

Their fins, needling puddles like broken
                seams,
   tack the moon to its curd reflection.

Our last dog was a snow scene. I still
                see her
    hemming trees, cleave to her
       frieze of subtle light.

VI

The forecast for St Swithins reminds me
of this. No diagnosis necessary.

At least I have an ending, of sorts.
Cutbacks curtail madness these days. She doesn't

approve. Nor of questions that imply a
danger to oneself. We have much in common.

Watch the same things. Wonder how to switch us off.

## This Tuesday's challenge: so you think you're a comedian

A mad dog and an Englishman go out in the midday sun.

You're nursing stitches and a fizzy drink. The next phone call rushes straight to your head, fries the rest of the afternoon. You'd like to watch a lizard skittle up a wall for its emerald eye, anything to wake this enforced siesta.

On the third stroke of heat the midday dog trails home, minus his sunman and a sombrero. When you see your face lapped in a mirror it has the same blue shimmer as the tiles on the bottom of a pool. You'd take your chances with a mosaic.

A gold lamé cliché pokes a head around a door.

*Don't be surprised*, it says, *if a naked man walks across this room.*

Someone else tells you there are beasts in the lagoon. You don't recognize the lettering on the shoreline. Maybe soon it will be way past your *bedtime.*

## How it ends

She's after taking the lid off to look inside, else hide her designer handbag. I give up my childhood but she's not having the books. I like that she's mad about horses, same as me (Spanish hair and accent for the last one). Lucky lavender brings out her eyes.

The session I leave my head at home, she's thrown, sitting there crying all day.

She won't catch me with that, too middle class, professional. There are always tissues. She works sideways, inside out. Serve her right if the others turn up, the sniveller, the seer, the one without a name. I have a right game with them in the dark, starless nights the most fatal.

Today I tell her it'll be years before I want to punch her in the face.

Something stillborn has left a trace behind her eyes. Elsewhere, another surprise, a baby lends its pre-natal miaow.

Don't tell me now how it ends.

## What you won't tell her

once you swallowed
the dictionary up all night
voiding your vowels *a*　　　　*e*　　　*i*　　　*o*

no point in school
after that you hook up
with red lettered days

dream a life more consonant
with the black typeface
you take to wearing out

the vellum of a muscular
prose pages crushed in
your hand blown *r*
　　　　　　　o　　　*s*
　　　　　　　　　　　　*e*　　　　．

## nightingale: symptomatic

in this version
aversion

to light therapy
h-a-p-p-y

visions of atonement
a mad

moment cured
of ague

bored with
raging

apathy
let's see

are you free next

| w | e | e | k | d | a | y | h | o | u | r | ? |
|---|---|---|---|---|---|---|---|---|---|---|---|
| w | e | e | k | d | a | y | h | o | u | r | ? |
| w | e | e | k | d | a | y | h | o | u | r | ? |
| w | e | e | k | d | a | y | h | o | u | r | ? |
| w | e | e | k | d | a | y | h | o | u | r | ? |
| w | e | e | k | d | a | y | h | o | u | r | ? |
| w | e | e | k | d | a | y | h | o | u | r | ? |
| w | e | e | k | d | a | y | h | o | u | r | ? |
| w | e | e | k | d | a | y | h | o | u | r | ? |
| w | e | e | k | d | a | y | h | o | u | r | ? |
| w | e | e | k | d | a | y | h | o | u | r | ? |

## Are you sitting comfortably?

I told her I was here for the craic.

*What's our aim?* she said. *You're level 4, complexandenduringneeds.*

Holy shit. How about a duplex in the desert? That cure it, you think? A rhyme
or two, on a screed of sand?

*Humour can be an effective Band-aid.*

Yeah, tried and tested.

*But not for ever, eh?* She smiles. I won't.

*Why not tell me about being arrested?*

Which occasion? Got all day? Caucasian female, middle age, full set of prints and DNA. Nothing more to say, your honour.   •   ●   ──
    '    ,    [full stop]



What made you think it would help?

## Sometimes, something, so what

First time she came it was with
a handful of Maltesers
pinched from Nana's sweetie tin.

Next it was a fist
and *dare do that again*.
It goes from this to torches

at the window, the night mob,
a plague on all your houses.
You get used to it.


Years she was dormant,
staked out in flame-coloured rags
and sudden corners,
sometimes print in snow,
blink of eye, roaring
of a field in flood.
Then the knocking of
heart against a door,
relentless, I let her in.


She's an accommodating
guest, if somewhat predictable.
Worst trait? The whimpering.

Next week I'm taking her to
anger management,
see how she likes that.

# Cataloguing catastrophe

**things that come in with weather**

make a winding sheet
of sky and treetops
abide (but not with me).
Inside, something

snow-soft stoppers
windows, floors: sudden
inhalation at a closing door.

**things lost**

Were they keepsake, precious, careless, theft?
Nothing left but a list:
animal, vegetable, mineral.
She is somewhere
in the middle.
Gracious.
Apart.

**things to climb into**

Place them wherever you like:
fishing creel, wardrobe,
cherry tree,
oak.
Stout boots. Fusty cloak.
They all wear the same smile.

**something to think about**

while you were sleeping
**owls called time on night,
sound a pebble of**
light at feathery glass.

## being accidental (in my mother's house)

some unspecified disorder
of flowers in a cracked vase
on the hall table eases me,

petals fluent in delinquent
gunmetal blues. Sunlight frets
the shock of them, unfamiliar

with their dialect. Water beads
collect at skirting and the hem
of her frock gathered for the fall.

## only nine words left

What if you ruined every syllable
with laughter, language too fulsome
for cariad evenings to bear to bed?

Isabelle says, *why not try
Italy for three months?*

Letters shake loose, as c o n   f   e   t      t         i
in m $_i$ n d   o f   a   ~~lych-gate~~, app l e s, s      k      y .
Th ere $_{are}$ al w a y s    ho r s e s ,  $_{sometimes}$    do g s.

Rain w   il  l       c  o  me  ·     Nig h t.

You     c o $_u$ld     ne $^v$ e $^r$    l $_i$ ve    he r e   .

## adventures with my house

I

The night the cat
dragged in I was
turquoising a pair
of remembered
earrings and your note
which said *italics*

*are catching*. All the
metallics in the
house were calling
but I have no truck
with knives: better
ways to chance luck,

lives I've yet to have
semi-quaver
baroque. The clock
was still ticking,
patio lights on —
tacky, ad hoc.

II

Beyond
the firewall
a front door

news from
the rialto.
Ope n   u  p  .

I    b   r   i   n    g
a  s  s   u  r  a  n  ces
the dead.

III

Something blew the roof off
its tiles a perturbation
constellation of teeth
tacked to a bro_ken ridge.

IV

What the kitchen wrote:

in my fridge
cheese
milk at ease
with itself.

Don't make a song and a dance of it.
**I have a moon** by the throat.

## No middle ground

What I know: nothing

she wears will fit me. Her dog dislikes rain. She's married, 25 years, holidays on the Broads, can sail, ride, doesn't do small talk. She'd be a therapist even if she won a million.

It's not much is it?

Once she worked a stud farm, up at 4 am, showered before muck-out, and, *perfume has been known*. Her dad used to lower her in the river, *off yer go*. She says *same-old, same-old, coo-k* (now I have her), *tell her get your own fucking dog*. They have a boat.

What I think I know: she is

pillow, feather, peony. I might meet her out of the blue. I was afraid of her in another life. She could be my friend in this. She is exact, lined with steel.

I cannot take her for human.

**the story of meeting a hero
on the occasion of his 51st birthday**

When the moon hits your eye
like a love boat on high
with a gondolier.
Back-street Romeo,
saucy as Dolmio,

bought for twenty lira.

da da da da dum
see his fingers strum
the lyre of a back
la la lack alack alack alack

.........

Rossini celebrates a full-throated
aria, lachrymose Ave Maria,
weeps at sunrise over the Duomo.

On a clearer day, in a cupola of bells,
when river's slack and all at sea,
he shaves, plenty of soap, rusty razor,

linguine of chin, cheeks, shape of
a radiccio-red tiara, and, further,
cries for the finest panini ever

eaten. At the opera, with the tenor,
feels the tremor of sudden tears, and,
not to be beaten, strains for the high notes,

causing both his eyes to water, the world
below him float away.      Volare.  O-oh.
Too much Campari.

Some say Rossini
was gay. What
do they know, pray?

# Lullaby

> Bass of rain on roof. Somewhere, sharp as fox, laughter, a man's voice drums a wall. Elsewhere, heels cymbal stairs, the electronic timpani of a security keypad, a receptionist's percussive signature calls.

**INSIDE**

> And the emotion?

It has no name.

I think it has. You mean none you care to give it?

> I have no name for it. I don't know its provenance, what country it inhabits.

> But you can navigate. You have your gene map.

> Oh that. What if I told you I'd thrown it away?

> I'd give you my copy. Or make you do it all again.

> Ooohh, taskmaster. Shall I throw a girdle about the world?

> Take your freedom where you will. No-one makes you stay.

[A chair sighs. Distant surf froths the window glass]

> Where are you now? [Hiss of silence] Rest there a while.

[Bone-crackle beyond the cranium]

> Stay, waiting.

[Imagine fur, the stroke of an ermine quill]

It still won't say what it is.

Don't tell me that. You have words. Aren't you supposed to be a writer?

« >:/ »

I haven't got a pen.

«Emote. Idiot»

Then give me a story. Lull me to sleep. What else would I never say? Aaah, yes; we have until dawn.

**way past your bedtime**

in a dusk-scuffed street kids kicking off kerbs
underneath the lamp-post by                        London

in a peculiar far-off lens time's telescope slopes
over the horizon the big ship sailed on

the alley alley o the o mio bab bi no ca ro crooning
a window, crackle of stars and static, lost stations,

Radio Luxembourg hisses Russian
all night this is London calling the world

## Think of it

*This is your space, not mine, to do with as you will. Think of it as a voyage*

All at sea and nothing
for miles save a forgotten history
basking on the horizon

somewhere in the lee
of tall ships racing
mariners sip

last syllables, syllabub
hub of a reeling Milky Way
oceanic bedtime in the drink

a cautionary tale this
voyaging to the brink
background orison only

a handkerchief of stars
barking on the quay

## For the journey

Think of it
                as a voyage
      gospel contained
                          by the light
                    of stars.
                In the hold
    of steerage
             a blue book
                                refrained
                       through the night
     stirs
                          a spice trail
                              to Zanzibar
              and cinnamon,
                       cardamom, murmurs
  in your ear.

Fear not.
       .   She shall
    be here.
                      And you
        still redolent of the hour.

# In (the) Hold

> The way silence,
> always canine,
>
> has texture, say
> a moleskin pelt,
>
> pitted walnut
> palmed across a yard,
>
> and permutations,
> ululated note.
>
> Treading port, starboard,
> phosphorescence
> breathes.
>
> I'm listening to
> the nuclear bones
>
> of an endless night
> dislocate, twice.
>
> For how does it
> begin? And when
>
> will it suffice?

## Stowed Away

You might well ask why
the fuss, that chiffon dress, the thickness
of a  s   i   g   h   exhaled in an airy room,
the groom a no-show,

bridal sheets idle and unmarked.
How rather than Miss Havisham
she ran away to sea, to be
a maritime highwayman, pirate,

pilot of her own star-struck steer,
down years robbing her blind
behind the pieces of hate,
swashbuckled *o-ho me heart is
                        over the ocean.*

                                            Don't
                                            call her
                                                Ishmael.

**Sidelined**

In the old days something
of cities, brutal gleam-
ing steel-gashed brick,

in your face glassed
towers, brackish flood of
people open all hours, back-

dropped, strangely gorgeous.
Inhabit edges now, forgotten
spaces devoid of buildings

you no longer read, avoid
all but where roads run out.
Not bitten by time, in dreams,

slow, susurration of tyres
on wet tarmac. Promised
snow you sleep, hands curled

against flecks of winter-north.
You wake to secrets, crystal
on the river's ice-bit flow.

# Drowning

In our version of
events she slept for

ever waking in
the aftermath of
a thunderstorm sky
bruised thumb, iridescent,

and across water
the whole month quiet,

figures, some human,
perished by a door,
others, at the mouth
of a leeward track,

too far gone, all
that light hammered

paper-thin across
her back, between the
eyes, come slinking home
like feral dogs, the

horizon spilled, ink,
indigo, and still

the river uncrossed,
many moons to go.

**how**

    some

                      *words*

         are themselves

          no

                         *more*

**revelations**

light's thousand faces
open hinges

geometric and unread


I know an atlas
whose fruit is

biblical, exorbitant


take me to the living
so say the seven

river-reivers


on my callused hand
tablets of stone

the rapture

**vascular**

Vasco da Gama, visionary, read
a muscular systolic thread
ravelled far around the globe,
of Leo's amber eye


Ravelled far around the globe,
old, perhaps before his time
in his fist an ancient rhyme
a lithograph of stars


Old and drunk on chartless time
sailed across the dragon line
in his fist an ancient rhyme
a lithograph in mourning

## immortality

No cartographer yet
found a rhyme among the
stars for bardic nights.

                              Mariners recite
                              last constellations
                             and sail on stellar

        inverse seas.

We drown
in lost iambic
light easy as she goes.

# astrolabe

of astronomical proportions
a libran warrior
concertinaed

paused by
Orion's star-bit hand

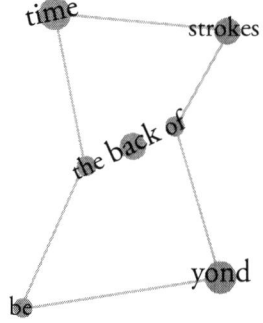

**lamentation**

missy a-dither

and skylightsdaubed

with dimmity's stain

fountain aflame

at window-glass

and all of us

go south! go south!


night burns up

in four-time driftandblue

and voices

ululu ululu

the tender's bell

for whom o for whom?

smaller s m a l l e s t

    i n   t h e   d a r k

                  h    a    r    k

**genesis**

                foetal drift

                of amnesiac stars

                oceans burn

                all night and

                in far-off

                fields fox-fired

                a gospel

                according

b    e    r    e    f    t

half-open
door without
lights on


the corpse road
extinguished
one by     one

# c h a p t e r s

coast track
spitting stars
pale as moths

its words
a kindling
of leverets

in a mouth

**reprise**

the world but

an hourglass

sifting blue

bones of light

through its hands

## Crossing an ocean, nightfall

    moon tranquill-
    izes summer   eye-
    let stars fasten
    needle-light
to ells
of cloud-
torn tulle
and un-
conscious or not
*it brings me back*
....

  an aesthetic
    of sorts
      and rough-
        stitched sailing
      *we are sailing*
                *across*
     a sky-blue
     bolt   irrevocable
     as singed hair
     and tide
     to salt in

the fabric
of our hearts

# Down

    in the auriole

                                              window a hole

        no bigger than

                                              Django's thumb

      a speck for birds

                                              to crumb at frost


          and here below

                                            no costly coat

       to throw

                                          a shoulder

            but Davy's locker

                                      without a lid


          I did nothing

                          wrong to bring me

        here but voices

                                  in an air

         at night

                    intimations


              beyond the light

## according to rain

*outside, at glass, rain  tick     tick        tick*
*who called you in? she asks,   dr$_i$$_p$     d$_r$$_i$$_p$*

*on glass fa$_l$$_l$i$^n$$^g$ in   out*

*no one calls you*
*p i t t e r  p a t t e r anymore,*
*offers umbrella for*
*a    $^r$ $_a$  $_i$ $_n$$_f$ $_a$ $_l$ $_l$*

             *which will d $_a$ $_y$  $_i$ $_n$  d $^a$ $^y$  $_o$ $^u$ $^t$*

**echo location**

man window Leintwardine
mo**o**n**ri**v**e**rseen
bide awhile? might you?


at the opera tenor
lemon twirl lemon twirl lemon
girl in a crystal which will
hear you tread ahead

of greening and foxes
breathing thus
o mio tango
with   the   dead


*here's the tender coming*
*off at Shiel's bar*
o  la la la   la di da da di dah
(get your own dog)


rain in her
rain in
out
a key

`GGGRRR GGRRUFF`

`RUFF`
`RUFF RUFF`

# Being of wonders

Like the boy from Billericay, five hundred year old gold reliquary seized from the skirts of an abandoned quarry. Beneath dirt and slurry names of the Magi engraved to its hilt. Lilt of lucre brought it in, father wondering why the bother for medieval treasure-tat, but pleased with knock-off leisure wear, flat plasma screens got with his share of the reward.
    At night brutal discord of his son's bad dreams, hoard of strange bejewelled shots: a pendant embossed and verdigris swinging in the wound of a hanging tree. Miasma blown from eastern lands, frankincense, myrrh, the upstrokes fur beneath his nails: Caspar, Melcior, Balthasar. Something burning in his hands: a desert rose, an ice-skald star.

I would like to tell you that

as a boy he doodled houses built on sticks
and lichen to last the cold, longed to live folded
in the crenellations of a castle, or on a farm,
waxing, excessively fond of potatoes.

He knew none of that,
was most frequently found strap-
hanging from rickety fire escapes
in the back of beyond, else smoking

through a gauze of tropical nights while
he watched lost satellites bobbing
on a liquid Milky Way.
Sometimes I'd meet him in limpid hotels,

the kind with a corsage of silky sheets,
where he'd split me like
a honeyed gourd with his visions
of atonement, how Walt Whitman raised

the dead, a montage of stories shelled
in the crimson of another day. And this,
how once, excavating the rubble
of a bombed-out building in Dresden,
he saw two men crouched over
what he thought was a china doll,
the memory of which caught him
slantwise and vertigo when his house
burned down one year on Ash Wednesday,
leaving him flung to an indigo sky,
in a tinnitus of dust, breath crushed
as the words on the tip of his tongue,
and nowhere else to go.

## Sailing a Calypso

What are guidebooks for without your way *around* a body?

She's hibiscus, sundog, dog star, Sirius. Your sign? Flat

line,  thin  line,  crippled  harlequin.

Cover her within an inch of life, skin a raglan knit for bone. Unhook the

fishtail

of her spine. She has sewn
herself to your exhaustion,
buttoned pagan light, an ocean.

# A different affair altogether

He said I've heard
of women who l i e
with cats.

I know of men
who l i e like dogs.
        Does that make u s   e v e n?

Perhaps in the end
that's all
it takes.

Later he would light
a river with the coldfire
of his s   t   e   p   s ,

libretto
on my skin.
I   s   a   n   g

to a different aria,
thin as mountain
air swimming

    through the lungs
      of ancient trees.
    Pleased, would I say?

There was nothing
  b  e  t  w  e  e  n    u  s
and the rest

of the day.
Something
about the faces

      on the opposite shore,
      their stealth.

    Declare yourself.

# In the lining of a pocket

                    not
           one of several stones
                    but
          singular, a sea-stain
      quartzed and quartered, criss-
                 crossed by
      stigmata in its river lines


                    not
           of this place or time
                    but
    hand-me-down, revelation,
            a last refrain
              crushed by
   weight of stardust in your bones


                 Follow. It
                 *will take*
                 *you home*
                 *Kathleen*
                 *to where*
                 voice-drift
                   -hark-
           on the starboard
                    rides

the moonless dark

**while I was thinking on**

the Italian for *lover* *amante*

a moon blooms in a garden

and river-song from open

throat drenching blossom

# Worlds Not Solid …

**on being captive**

∫ how I was taken
before their leader,
queen, blue of eye and face

held of little esteem,
compelled to bow, to scrape,
to sleep upright between

pillar, post, as though
a fellow disgraced,
I of family known

in Leintwardine and
mountains black, heir to
rivers, rain, runic lore …

I digress, Your Grace,

                              forgive.

∫ of how I came to live
in this place…; here — the book.

Not crook, nor felon,
highwayman, though having

been this way before,
yet more. Might you bide

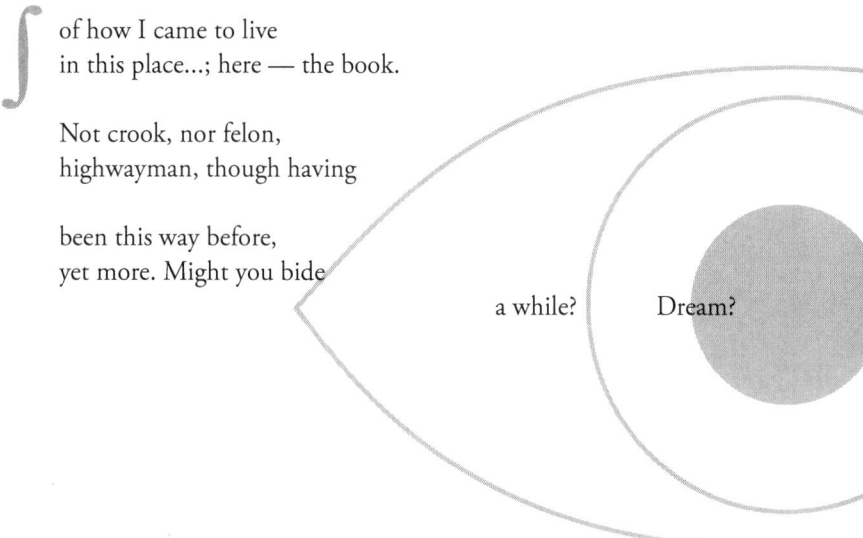

a while?    Dream?

**on how I mended my ways**

∫ this in a year I was learning to tango & a man
fell from the sky, pumpkin moons out of season,
such disorder was there in earth's twist and tilt.

∫ One night, taken to the river in my cups &
the white-tip-tailed fox tiptoed across the bridge,
I met my mother in a fable, she, not mink-stoled,
moth-balled, but in a cashmere kind of coat
unbuttoned to elements though trees were
scoundrel in a coming storm.

∫ She, Muscovy's breath beneath her shadow,
opened hands to palms of stones, small, bone-white —
perhaps they were — & proffered on this rutted track.

∫ Afeared to take one lest at last I find
my name, I stood in fielding ribs, half-cut
ahead of Greening & wordless she,
one of us — perhaps me — no footprints
leavening a tread, so that come morning
I knew this, an admonition from the dead …

**on finding treasure**

∫ Be it bullion, pearl, or artefact
the trick is to discard what's mapped;
So say I this in Year of Lark.

Hearken, be you king or churl,
for this befell one summer's eve
as sleepless I in rumination
startled by a declaration.

Full soft it was, as listless sigh
at window flung to heaven's eye.

Curious, I laid aside my book
& to the balcony came to look.

∫ & summoned thus
on eagle's back,
as feathered cushion
from a lap I flew
on high & slumbered
fast, at last to dream.

∫ So now of all the treasures seen on earth
below & soaring realms of phantasy
which my guide did spell for me.

∫ Here and there, on the pillars of an air,
melody, resounding note, of Hottentot
& Huguenot, secret worlds where rivers
slow replete and dread.

∫ And when I woke
upon my bed
rubies on the
coverlet spread.

All this is truth.
& what is more,
coming through the
dawn I saw a ...

# Keys

and not
a lock
to open

doormoonstar
fieldseasky
n i g h t r i v e r s o n g

long this voyage

oceanwindow
homecomesail

all the meadows
wringing
in the light

# I saw you walking (Sky field)

scent of May and hay spread and
stooked in meadow-sweet stubble.
Heat-pricked skin, soles of feet

blush at earth's vibrato,
tingling bird, insect, wildflower.
The hour shimmers blue, remembered.

Something speaks you from within.

# Home

another morning fled
through the back door
   and still

  you're waiting
 to be named
     light a river

   rushing out
 a spill of peonies
  in your hands

   the upstairs window
  a lighthouse
   churning distance

    far-off fields
   sky a linen lawn
      unfolding and everything

    so much smaller
     than you remember

# What rain taught us

I

Forty nights, and still no sight
of land.

Ghost-bone moon stands in
for northern lights.

In another life, clouds make
rosaries of the wind.

Trees sing. Long days
green as fire.

These maps have
done for us.

Hearts go out,
one by one.

II

We are salt-sheet sailors full hardy.
Hardly a day passes without a storm.

Our faces on the horizon opening
doors calling the weather in.

We watch it come. Time will run us down,
leather-whipped dogs. B  e   c  a  l  m.

A ship of **fools** might stay us.

III

Moonlight frangipanes trees.
We dream of nights such as these,
balmy air's calypso hum,

cicadas shaking sea-legs
to a ration of rum rum rumba.
Women soft as the dregs

of rain-silked kisses latino
out the light. Cartographers
tell of Americas

north and south. When she traces
a lifeline through my mouth,
I am put in mind of the breeze.

IV

Though miles inland
fields are maritime
brined in sea-shot
waves of light, and still

no sextant, chart,
or course to fathom
ocean's salt-stinged
cry, these **black**-backed stars,

slow migration
through empty chambers
of a tidal heart.

You steer by touch
and sailors' luck,
life a continent
of somewhere else —

lo! exotic fruit,
miracle beasts,
cutlass, Prester John.

We might wish ourselves
a distant surf,
voyage     yet     to     come.

**singing bowl (copper, tonal)**

is a ickle lickle ting
hear im on de tang and riddim of de wind

im slippin here loose-limbed water
mi slicky shiny licky limboed daughter

brim o light she windin
upstairs downstairs in mi lady's chamber

no one ever name her calypso
no ever name her fly she go

everywhere a rainbow sing  sing    sing    sing
everywhere a rainbow sing

## in a room full of lost objects

Once the room
was lost to sea

it was something
to tuck in the bag

beneath the bed with
the other lives, songs

you might inhabit,
shanties more sallow

in the dark than you
recall, each *blow blow*

*blow the man down* and
out of nowhere it

came flooding back, how
you kept a stillborn

moon in a bowl on the
sideboard, its struck note

copper, tonal, and
even now — the eyes

are yours — her face in
every upturned spoon.

**a face in every upturned**

                                          raindrop of light up
                                    ended in an angel's hand
                                    makes prayers of us all

# Book of Hours

*For Michelle*

**gingerbread house**

no telling
what's inside
save the bed

room in the eaves
astonished mouth
of a fireplace

**but worlds and time**

I have known this
in so many

places, skin
of other

skies, north, east,
and more, lit by

heaven's silk,
stars outraged.

Our breath will spin
bridges from air.

Ropes of glass
hold us there.

*circumlocution*

*For the world is round
and many of us
have its shape thereof:
orb, hull, crown of skull,
the circular flush
of a hallowed moon.*

*You have followed me
all the way. There is
yet time, more to say.*


*keep*

*How to speak a heart
orbital, oblique.*

*Things we cannot keep
call us home. Come, sleep.*


*back, again*

*The house smoking
on the horizon.
I see you now*

*booted, gloved
unlock a door
too stiff to yield.*

*Behind us
flotilla of fields,
a single deer.*

# Nothing short (of miraculous)

And once the sleeve
of a shrugged-off
coat slaps you,

there's no telling
how it will end,
the pelt of astonishment

how a furred tongue might
feel against your skin
at the exact moment

(far off yet distinct
as a dripping tap
against a Belfast sink)

someone flings a voice
from a window:
*now is the time to open*

*your heart.* When it falls
at your feet it can go *either*
*way.*

# History of the world

                    you carry it in
                    your pocket

                cat's cradle   bone
                perhaps a marble's

                    cobalt eye
                    sometimes

                a skeletal whale
                held up to light

                  islands ridge
                  its spine   worlds

              a former sigh and ozone

---

*[On the left side of the page, printed in mirror-reversed text:]*

**Apparently**

The time I log out
with my fractured wrist

she tells me writing
with the left hand will

access my inner
child. Is this the same

one that sits minding
its business, mannered?

We're good at it, me
and her. The rose quartz

crystal hanging by
a thread at open

windows knows it. And
the scratching of a

closing door, the stifled
sobs of her shoe-prints,

receding